LA
CIT
AMO

L'Art de Vivre

BELLES DEMEURES DE PARIS

BEATON

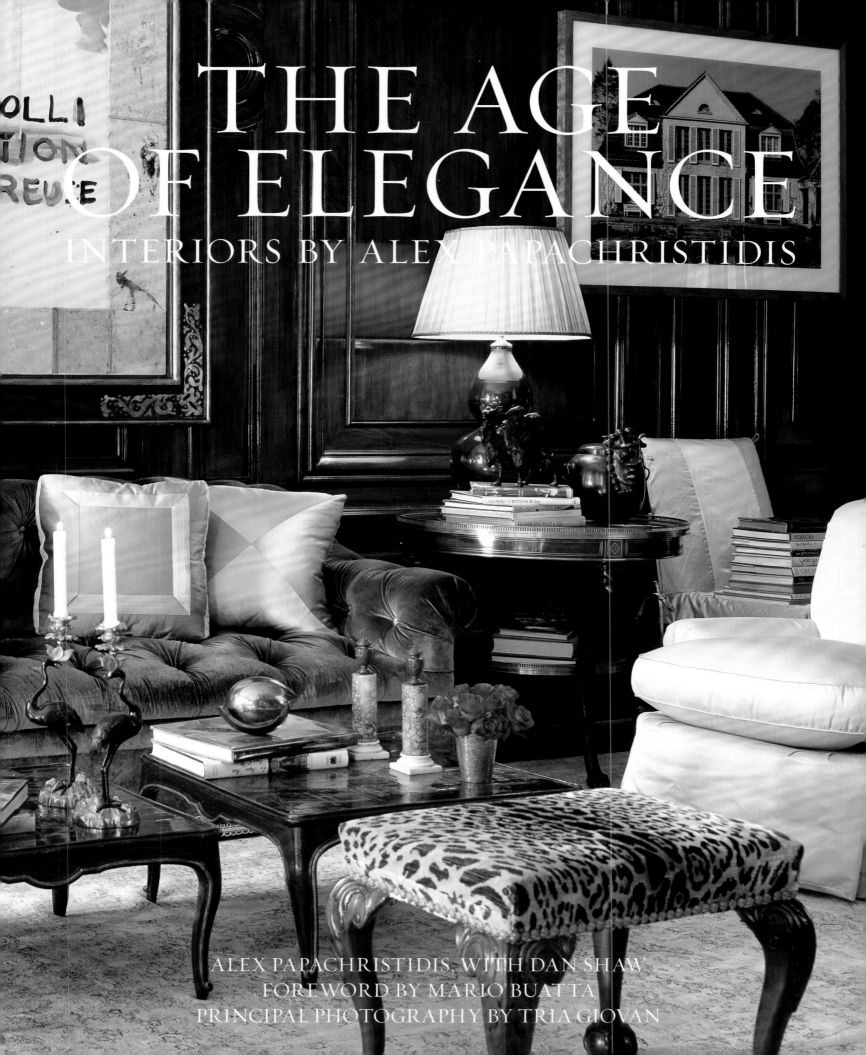

THE AGE
OF ELEGANCE

INTERIORS BY ALEX PAPACHRISTIDIS

ALEX PAPACHRISTIDIS, WITH DAN SHAW
FOREWORD BY MARIO BUATTA
PRINCIPAL PHOTOGRAPHY BY TRIA GIOVAN

TO MY MOTHER, MARIYA, A WOMAN
WITH AN AWE-INSPIRING SENSE OF
STYLE AND JOIE DE VIVRE, WHO TOOK
ME ALL OVER THE WORLD AND EXPOSED
ME TO THE WONDERS OF LIFE.

CONTENTS

FOREWORD
by Mario Buatta

Alex Papachristidis's work is very thoughtful, very personal, and very livable. It looks as though people actually live in his rooms. His style is charming and eclectic, and he has a knack for making rooms feel as if they've been there for a long time. He puts different periods together, mixing contemporary and traditional in a way that looks cozy and comfortable. His work has a sense of history, which I appreciate. There are not many designers today who do what he does.

Like me, he's detail oriented, which I respect. He knows his antiques, and he does wonderful things with trims and fabrics. I don't like rooms that look as though they were put together in six weeks—or six months. I like a room to look as if it's been there for a long, long time and evolved over several generations. Nowadays, it's harder to find good antiques unless you are decorating with mid-century, but Alex does. His rooms are very thought out, and that requires time, which can be tough for clients who want everything done yesterday.

A good decorator brings out his clients' personalities. Most of them don't know what they want, but if you show it to them and teach them, they will get excited and involved. Alex's rooms look as though they belong to clients who've been educated—people who *care*. He does a very nice job of setting the stage for them to act out their lives. He understands that people will inherit things, buy things, and collect things. He knows they will add to and subtract from his rooms, which is what living is all about.

Besides being talented, he is a gentleman who exudes warmth and caring. He's got a great smile—and he loves people and dogs. He comes from a big, friendly family and that shows in his work, suggesting the great English country houses that get their character from being family homes passed down through generations. If I weren't a decorator myself, I would hire him.

OPPOSITE: "Shangri-La" was the name of the 2000 Kips Bay Show House bedroom I created with Toni Raeymaekers, my former partner and still very dear friend. The seating area featured sofas upholstered in a tree-of-life Braquenié with an antique Uzbek draped over an arm. The magnificent Dutch mirror over the fireplace was from Florian Papp.

INTRODUCTION

There's no more important place in the world than your own home. Whether you live alone or with children, in-laws, assorted pets, and a spouse, your home should reflect your personality and soothe your soul. Having traveled all over the world, I've been awed and dazzled by the sites I've seen and places I've visited, but the site that inspires and touches me the most with its beauty is my own home. My joy in coming home is not a sentimental reflex; I've put a lot of thought, time, and energy into how I live, and I am rewarded every day by my effort. I put the same amount of thought and care into my clients' happiness and comfort.

I was taught the value of living well by my parents. My Canadian mother has always been an Auntie Mame figure—super glamorous, intelligent, and charming. My Greek father was imposing and very much a gentleman of the old school. They were aesthetes with high standards. Good manners were very important to them, but so was enjoying life and experiencing the world on every level. They exposed me to so much—museums, art, theater, travel—that I developed an insatiable curiosity and a far-reaching continental sensibility.

We moved constantly in Manhattan (though once my mother took us to Greece for the summer, and we stayed for two years), which may explain why I empathize with clients confronted with an empty space that they want to turn into a home. I grew up discussing the decoration of our apartments with my mother. Although she loves antiques and old-world luxury, we always lived in brand-new buildings: She never liked to live where anyone had

OPPOSITE: For the Kips Bay Show House "Shangri-La" bedroom, Jane Holzer lent us the Warhol portrait of Elizabeth Taylor that hangs over the custom bed upholstered in Braquenié. A Queen Anne secretary from Kentshire made for a fabulous night table. The graphic stenciled floors were by the incomparable Andy Holland.

already lived. We always had apartments on high floors with wonderful light and views but lacking in inherent charm or architectural presence. As a result, my mother's uncanny ability to mix antiques and modern furnishings has been essential in giving them an elegance that reflects her stylish sensibility and made us feel at home.

Like the French furniture and modern art that made her heart race, my mother is formidable, and her zest for living has always been infectious. We are a very close family—consisting of my parents, my sisters, and a brother who have all supported my decorating career. I spent a lot of time with my mother as she made the rounds of shops and galleries to furnish our homes. Once people met her, they never forgot her, and to this day, people in the antiques business always ask me how she is. She has always been impeccably dressed and loves beautiful clothes, so for the longest time I thought I might go into the fashion business because I had the eye and the vocabulary from all the time I spent shopping with her.

But it turned out, I was not really cut out for life on Seventh Avenue; nor was I a great fit for the family's international shipping business I was expected to enter. Then, in a stroke of inspiration, my childhood friend Laura Broumand hit upon the perfect career for me. I had finished college, and we were sitting in my first apartment when she said, "Alex, you have such great taste—you should be a decorator." It was a brilliant suggestion, because decorating is a profession that combines my passions for beauty and for bringing people joy. It's a genteel field that allows me to interact with sophisticated, artistic individuals on a daily basis, allowing me to be my best self.

My sister Ophelia was my first big client. She and her husband, Bill, were moving to a large apartment on Park Avenue, and she'd been interviewing some of New York's most respected interior designers. Finally, she came to me and said, "Why would I want to use a stranger to decorate my home? Why don't *you* do it?" It was an ambitious assignment and life-changing opportunity. My sister has her own very personal sense of style, yet she believed in me 100 percent and I have been decorating homes for her, Bill, and my niece, Samantha, and nephew,

Michael, ever since. As I write this, I am putting the final touches on her new apartment. Her faith and loyalty have meant everything to me.

There are three other women who have played an integral role in my career. My first business partner was Leslie Anderson. It was just the two of us in the early years; we'd do all the decorating together and then she'd go home and type the invoices at night. Eventually, she got married and started raising children in Connecticut, and her life got so busy that when she and her husband built their new home in Greenwich, she tapped me to be their decorator. After Leslie, I hired the fabulously stylish Fruzsina Keehn to be my right hand. We shared a sensibility and became best friends. After a few years, she moved to England to pursue a career as a jewelry designer, and she brought me to London to help decorate her flat. Eventually, I took on another partner, Toni Raeymaekers, who helped me expand my business into what it is today. We collaborated blissfully for eight years until she decided to get remarried and move to Europe.

For a long time, even after these women were no longer my colleagues, I kept "Anderson, Papachristidis, Raeymaekers" as the name of the firm so they would know the door was open if they ever wanted to come back. But eventually it became clear that they had moved on for good, and I decided to change the name of the firm to Alex Papachristidis Interiors. I vowed that I would never take on another business partner because I couldn't bear losing one ever again—it's too emotional.

My passion for elegance makes me a very traditional decorator in many respects. I am drawn to the eighteenth century, when some of the greatest furniture ever designed was made. To my mind, even the best modern furniture references eighteenth-century shapes and silhouettes, which have a classic, timeless quality. I like to layer historical elements into every interior because if everything is new, a home can only have a superficial charm, and I believe a home should have depth of character. My approach is in its own way very old school as well: I like to have a relationship with everything in a home, so it is filled with conversation pieces—things that possess not only style but also stories. I have to sit in a chair and touch a piece of fabric before making a decision about a purchase.

LEFT: A painting by Southampton gallery owner Mark Humphrey hangs over a Louis XVI fruitwood desk at my 2006 Hampton Designer Show House room, "La Chambre du Jardin Chinois." The Scandinavian clock is from Dienst + Dotter. OPPOSITE: A chalky-white bed from Robert Lighton is dressed in fabric from Lee Jofa. The knockout blue-and-white painted floor is by Andy Holland.

My office and home are overflowing with books on art and design. I have studied, analyzed, and absorbed the work of many legendary designers such as Sister Parish, Georges Geffroy, Renzo Mongiardino, Billy Baldwin, Elsie de Wolfe, John Fowler, and Emilio Terry. My style icons include Pauline de Rothschild, Mona Bismarck, and the Duke and Duchess of Windsor. Their unique sensibilities have inspired me to cultivate my own.

A great interior should be beautiful and usable. One of my core beliefs is that living rooms are for living. They should not be rooms that you merely pass through. They're usually the most expansive and divine room in any house, so it's important that they be enjoyed. I always try to put a card table or television in the living room because these pieces draw you in and encourage you to use the room. A games table is good for so many activities, and it's a romantic place to dine *à deux* instead of in the dining room or kitchen. Another major living space is the master bedroom. For me, the bed is always the focal point of this peaceful sanctuary. My beds are lush and comfortable pieces of furniture.

I am not big on "rules" per se, but I am a stickler for details, and you will notice that every

lampshade, pillow, and curtain is trimmed with a carefully chosen gimp, tape, or fringe. Getting the balance right in any interior requires a layering of materials and textures: There needs to be a combination of matte and shimmer, light and heavy, solids and patterns. I never have a plain-skirted sofa; mine always have wonderful carved feet or a generous fringe. One of my favorite things to do is to mix painted, upholstered chairs with wood dining tables. I like rooms to have a collected feel, which means I keep matched sets (except for sconces, bedside lamps, and dining room chairs) to a minimum—a room should not look like a "pair party." There is not a lot of recessed lighting in the rooms that I design. I prefer chandeliers, hanging lanterns, and the warm glow of standing lamps and table lamps with silk or cotton shades.

My decoration of a home is never finished. It evolves as my clients live in it. I am often called back to hang art or reupholster a chair, and invariably I start rearranging things, and a housekeeper will say: "I don't think you should touch that." But in truth, I can't help it, and the clients are always glad for it. And that's the method to my madness: I treat their homes with care and thought, as if they were my own.

GRAND WHIMSY

You can't be timid when you're decorating a large house. You need to be brave, bold, and emphatic. When you have acres of space, the gutsy choice is usually the right one, which is why this house has so many eye-popping fabrics with robust character and amply proportioned pieces of furniture that make a statement without overwhelming any room.

I had already worked with this couple on other projects in New York and London when they decided to build a house in Southampton, New York. I introduced them to architects Anne Fairfax and Richard Sammons, who have established a thriving practice by designing new houses that look as if they've always been there. I was certain that Fairfax & Sammons would create a home that was right not only for Long Island but also for this couple, who did not want a typical shingled "cottage." Having grown up in the South, the wife was partial to plantation architecture, which is why she wanted the house to possess a formality that harkens back to more genteel and gracious times. She loves old-school decorating with all the bells and whistles, and we agreed that vivid colors and lively patterns would be essential components of the decor.

Fortunately, there is a comfort level between us that comes from having worked together for nearly twenty years, so she was willing to trust me when I suggested grand gestures. Moreover, there was the convenience of my knowing what pieces of furniture she owned that we might "borrow" for the new house, such as the nineteenth-century red lacquer chinoiserie secretary that we'd bought at auction in New Orleans some fifteen years ago and used in both her New York and London homes. It was a key piece of the Southampton living room because it represents her sense of whimsy, her appreciation of quality, and our shared belief that a beautifully decorated house should always make you smile.

OPPOSITE: A David Hicks chinoiserie wallpaper was a daring choice for the enormous foyer. The carpet on the double staircase is from my line for Beauvais; the pattern is called Scott's Chevron. The octagonal hall table has a skirt fashioned from a paisley batik. The big majolica shell is one of many red accents throughout the house.

16

ABOVE: The house designed by Fairfax & Sammons for my clients has magnificent proportions and spectacular light. OPPOSITE: A pair of Chinese Chippendale chairs flank a George III gilt-wood console in the paneled foyer. The églomisé paintings of Turks are from Alidad in London. The neoclassical urns are majolica.

18

RIGHT: The living room has three distinct seating groups with exuberant upholstery: At one end of the room, the sofa is covered in a classic Brunschwig & Fils pattern featuring pheasants and flowers; the armchairs were designed to show off an extraordinary piece of needlepoint I found with dolphins and foliage; the velvet poufs, which I bought at auction, are trimmed in passementerie with ikats sewn onto the tops. The blue-and-cream-striped silk curtains have a red bullion fringe and velvet trim. As a warm counterpoint to all the color, I had cream-and-tobacco wool rugs woven in India for each seating group. There are matching eighteenth-century Dutch brass chandeliers, which we bought in Paris, at both ends of the room.

ABOVE: In front of the fireplace, the living room's central seating group includes two custom-
made tufted slipper chairs in velvet-striped paisley; they are big enough for two, which makes
them especially wonderful for entertaining. In a big room like this, you want furniture that
can be moved around, such as the Georgian chair with flame-stitch upholstery and the
eighteenth-century French chair that's upholstered in both gaufrage linen and an elaborate
paisley. The blue tufted sofa has red velvet buttons and trim. OPPOSITE: I painted the big English
Gainsborough chair a chalky white and upholstered it in a snappy plaid. The nineteenth-
century English chinoiserie secretary was bought at auction in New Orleans many years ago.

ABOVE: In the dining room, a tea-stained chinoiserie wallpaper from Scalamandre is hung above the chair rail. I designed the upholstered buffet that's trimmed in French nailheads. OPPOSITE: The Schumacher ikat curtains with pagoda valances push the Far East theme to dazzling dimensions. The tole chandelier is decorated with leaves and flowers. The client bought the table in London, and I paired it with English chairs in the French manner that are painted a chalky white and green. Instead of a carpet, I had the floors stenciled in a pattern inspired by style icon Pauline de Rothschild's bedroom in London.

LEFT: The master bedroom features a sumptuous bed that I designed and upholstered in Braquenié fabric from Pierre Frey. The walls are covered in creamy striae wallpaper from Cowtan & Tout. The aqua silk curtains are trimmed in velvet with bamboo blackout shades beneath. The gilt-wood sunburst mirror is nineteenth century. I custom-colored the small-patterned carpet for Beauvais, which was woven in India. For nightstands, I used a painted Louis XV table on one side and a Maison Jansen commode on the other.

WEST SIDE GLAMOUR

There's a mythology surrounding New York's classic apartment buildings from the 1920s and 1930s, which suggests they all have gracious layouts, wonderful moldings, and perfect proportions. Alas, it's not true. But I love myths—I am Greek after all!—and I like nothing better than gutting an apartment and giving it the bones it should have had in the first place. My collaborators on this project were the classical architects Fairfax & Sammons. We took what had been a typical family apartment on Central Park West, where all the rooms had been railroaded down a hallway, and transformed it into an incredibly sophisticated one-bedroom apartment.

The decorating has a French '40s feel that's luxe and masculine, which is meant to showcase the detailed but clean architecture and highlight the magnificent views of the park. The paneled entrance hall has a contemporary attitude because it is painted all one color, and the graphic circle-and-square-stenciled floors have a similarly modernist aesthetic. The geometry is echoed in the dining room's coffered ceiling, which became a way not only to hide some load-bearing beams but also to give the room its robust character. Besides a table that seats ten and a pair of one-sided sofas flanking the fireplace, there's a games table by the window, where the owners often have breakfast. It's truly multipurpose—my favorite type of room.

Obviously, one of the best parts of working with open-minded architects from the get-go is that you're able to solve problems together, which can lead to innovation. For instance, we designed a niche in the guest bedroom that was exactly the dimensions of a queen-size bed. I imagined a daybed bedecked with pillows for lounging, but since it would be used for sleeping, too, we put the bed on casters so it can be easily made up—a fabulous melding of form and function.

OPPOSITE: With its graphic stenciled floors, the foyer has an understated grandeur that comes from mixing ornate elements such as the Swedish Egyptian Revival commode and a nineteenth-century neoclassical chandelier with sparer, modern pieces—a 1940s mirror from the Paris flea market and a 1960s glass and brass lamp.

RIGHT: Every piece in the living room, such as the spectacular twentieth-century mahogany and brass Italian desk, has its own strong character, but taken together they exude a sense of restrained elegance. The custom light fixture above the fireplace is made of brass and glass with a silk shade. The silk taffeta curtains are on custom gilt bronze poles.

OPPOSITE: The squares on the twentieth-century French cabinet correspond to the foyer floors. The neoclassical coffee table with ram's heads and saber legs has a leather top. It sits on a Tibetan wool rug. The custom sofa is upholstered in cotton velvet with satin throw pillows. ABOVE: I like order and symmetry, but too much can be monotonous, which is why I created different vignettes on either side of the French nineteenth-century marble mantel: On the left, there's a Swedish cabinet with a 1970s wall sculpture; on the right, there's a simple parchment table with a biomorphic brass lamp. The neoclassical twentieth-century bergères are upholstered in an abstract cotton print that reads like cheetah spots. The painting over the fireplace is by Cynthia Knott.

33

ABOVE: The niche was designed in collaboration with the architects to accommodate a queen-size mattress for guests, which is dressed as a daybed with pillows in velvet, wool, and Fortuny. The walls are upholstered in cognac-colored brushed wool. OPPOSITE: In the dining room, the coffered ceiling repeats the geometric leitmotif that extends throughout the apartment. The mahogany table is twentieth-century Scandinavian, and the rosewood chairs are American. There is no chandelier because the table is not centered in the room. There are nickel picture lights over the bookcases, and swing-arm lamps on the back wall provide additional illumination. The painting over the fireplace is by Ryan McGinness.

A CONNOISSEUR'S COLLECTIONS

It's always gratifying when a client shares my zeal for the decorative arts, but it's especially rewarding when he has a passion for decorating itself. After seeing one of my Kips Bay Show House rooms, a friend who collects English furniture and neoclassical antiques asked if I would help him with his apartment. He made it very clear that he was not afraid to take risks and push boundaries. He was determined to be daring, and I was more than happy to encourage him! This project was a true meeting of the minds.

Although he has a great eye, he needed someone to help him curate his choices and stay focused on the big picture. He wanted to surround himself with beautiful things, but he was wary of his home looking like a museum. We collected together, and when he went shopping on his own he would usually send me a photograph before making a purchase. For instance, he conferred with me before bidding on a highly unusual contemporary gilt-wood and Madagascan rock-crystal tree-form side table by Gabhan O'Keeffe, the London designer who's known for his fantasias, which was being auctioned at Sotheby's. Without hesitation, I said, *"Go for it."* I thought it would not only fit in with all of the serious antiques but also add a dash of humor to what might otherwise become too formal a room.

The client already had the big tufted sofa upholstered in the iconic gold-and-blue Dragon Empress brocade from Clarence House, which became the basis for the sumptuous living room. To keep everything approachable, I was very deliberate in choosing a low-key background, so the walls are painted the color of wheat and the floors are covered in sisal. It was essential to maintain the

OPPOSITE: A vignette centered on an English gilt-wood console in the living room reflects the client's cosmopolitan aesthetic: There's a modern painting, an African mask, a bronze Persian pitcher, and a contemporary lamp by Christopher Spitzmiller. A marble silhouette in a Dutch frame hangs on the wall. There is a modern brass sculpture resting on a stack of books below.

The books on the table read:

THE GIVENCHY STYLE
DELFTWARE
TAMAYO

PRECEDING SPREAD: I designed the Venetian-style sofa with gilt finials and cut-velvet upholstery so that it would have as much presence as any of the antiques, especially the Regency scroll bench upholstered in horsehair from Louis Bofferding. The modern elements that give the room its unorthodox edge include the gilt and rock-crystal table by Gabhan O'Keeffe, the abstract painting by Cleve Gray, and the bronze sculpture by Beverly Pepper.
OPPOSITE: A Chinese terra-cotta horse is a bit of whimsy atop a regal eighteenth-century English secretary.
ABOVE: An eighteenth-century neoclassical Italian painting hangs over the tufted sofa that the client brought with him from his previous apartment. The Swedish Etruscan chairs with nailhead trim came from the estate of Bill Blass.

balance between dressy and casual, so there are matchstick blinds beneath the golden linen curtains that are trimmed in an open wool braid.

The apartment manages to feel contemporary because it blends modern and traditional motifs in an uninhibited way. To my mind, neoclassical things—whether French, Russian, or Swedish—never look dated, and they can be combined in endless variations. It's the mix of modern art with ornate furniture that is so sophisticated and soigné: the pairing of a leopard-print-upholstered eighteenth-century gilt chair with a Beverly Pepper bronze sculpture that looks like an African figure; the abstract Cleve Gray painting hanging over the Venetian-style sofa that I designed and upholstered in cut velvet; the bold, geometric Alexander Liberman painting that hangs on the dining room wall alongside a collection of blue-and-white Chinese and Delft porcelain.

It was important to the client that the apartment feel masculine, and the library reflects his interest in history and hunting. Like a European gentleman's smoking room, it's seriously plush with a tiger-stripe-patterned carpet and antlers hung on walls covered in a paper that looks like leather. A pair of Turkish ottomans sit under a deer-leg table from the estate of Bill Blass, adding an air of well-bred bohemia.

The master bedroom is suitably suave and urbane. To my mind, the bed must be a serious piece of furniture—as important as the sofa is to the living room—and this one draws you in with its paisley headboard and footboard with a skirt trimmed in a thick eight-inch fringe. Dressed with custom sheets, an antique Indian bedspread, and a fox throw, the bed is as layered and luxurious as every other room of the collector's home.

PRECEDING PAGES: The silk taffeta curtains hang from a modified pagoda valance made of the same striae velvet used on the chairs. The gilt settee is Regency. The custom dog bed is one of several in the apartment. A Maison Jansen crystal chandelier hangs over the dining room table that's covered in a wool tapestry from Brunschwig & Fils. The Venetian chairs have cushions made of cotton striae velvet. The wallpaper is a subtle trellis pattern that showcases the graphic painting by Alexander Liberman. The life-size gilt ostrich from H. M. Luther is the ultimate conversation piece. OPPOSITE: In the library, custom-made ottomans are kept under a Victorian-style mahogany and white-painted table with hoofed legs from the estate of Bill Blass. The mahogany Georgian bookcase has a lighted coral interior and on top there's a collection of "grand tour" Greek urns.

RIGHT: In the library, a Regency mirror hangs over a sofa upholstered in velvet and cut-up pieces of Braquenié fabric. A tiger-stripe-patterned carpet and walls papered to look like leather provide a masculine sensibility. The red lacquered chinoiserie coffee table has a subtle gold band. The collection of antlers adds to the clubby atmosphere.

46

ABOVE: A marble bust and framed collection of Roman gold seals are flanked by curtains made from a Hodsoll McKenzie fabric with stylized birds. OPPOSITE: The custom headboard and footboard are upholstered in a cotton paisley, and the skirt is trimmed in a bullion fringe. The bed is made with custom Schweitzer linens, an antique Indian bedspread, and a fox throw. Gilt-mounted oxblood ceramic lamps have silk plaid shades. The carpet is a trellis pattern from Stark.

ABOVE: A nineteenth-century box made of wax seals, a bronze of Caesar, and marble pillars with gilt bronze eagles are displayed on a Louis XVI commode from H. M. Luther. OPPOSITE: Neoclassical Swedish chairs upholstered in gaufrage velvet look right with a neoclassical Russian bookcase that holds a pair of nineteenth-century French vases and a marble bust of Caesar.

EDUCATED STYLE

It's a luxury to have all the space you could ever imagine, but it's also challenging to create a cozy, family atmosphere on a grand scale. There's a serious risk that a big house will look like a small hotel if it's not filled with enough one-of-a-kind antiques and more than a few dramatic flourishes. When you start with impeccable architecture and stunning views of Long Island Sound, you need to be especially conscientious and respectful: The furniture must be as well wrought as the moldings and coffered ceilings, and the colors must complement the abundant natural light, from dawn to dusk, in every season.

My former business partner and her husband built their dream house in Greenwich, Connecticut, which ended up larger than they ever expected. She asked me to help her keep the house from becoming grand, for her style is casual and low-key. The seaside location made things tricky because the light changes so dramatically, which meant that figuring out the exact right colors for the walls was going to be important. Thus, we turned to internationally renowned color consultant Donald Kaufman, who's known as the "poet of pigments." He helped us select the perfect watery aqua for the foyer, the ideal creamy white for the living room, a warm taupe that's the color of sand for the dining room, and an earthy tobacco for the family room. It's a nuanced palette that's in harmony with the spectacular New England setting. The elaborately paneled living room is painted a single shade, which is a great way to make a traditional room feel modern. Comfortable and easy to enjoy, the house has a casual, happy, sophisticated feeling that not only suits the owners' needs but also reflects their understated style.

OPPOSITE: A skirted hall table in a striae cotton with wool fringe adds warmth to the foyer with its limestone floors. An antique Georgian bench upholstered in horsehair is placed by the staircase, which has a geometric sea-foam wool runner. OVERLEAF: The all-white living room is a multifunctional space with a games table, where the owners play bridge, and a piano, where the children take music lessons. The custom rug is shaggy, adding a cozy layer. Although the room has little color, the variety of furniture shapes provides dramatic interest. The curtains are tree-branch sheers that filter the natural light. The painting over the fireplace is by Robert Kelly, and the light fixture is by Fortuny.

PRECEDING PAGES: In the chocolate-brown library, wool felt walls and a custom velvet mohair sofa with pillows by Holland & Sherry frame a bay window with spectacular views. The modern aqua leather and brass chairs are from Soane in London, which makes new furniture that is destined to be tomorrow's antiques. The Chinese lantern echoes the bay window in a theatrical fashion. In the dining room, an eighteenth-century Dutch chandelier hangs over an antique mahogany table surrounded by chairs from Liz O'Brien that are based on the designs of Samuel Marx, the influential Chicago architect. An eighteenth-century English highboy handsomely fills the niche next to the fireplace.

LEFT: A custom carpet incorporating brown, aqua, and cream sets the palette for the family room, which shows off the neo-traditional style of architect Dinyar Wadia. The custom sofas and armchairs surround a table made from reclaimed wood by the late Amy Perlin. The wicker chairs from Bielecky Brothers have cushions in a green-and-aqua floral print by Michael Smith that was also used for throw pillows. The curtains are an apple-green batik, and the chandelier is a custom design in silk, bronze, and glass by Metamorphosis.

OPPOSITE: I love four-poster beds because they create instant atmosphere, and when I dress them I often keep the curtains off the end of the bed to give a more open feeling. Here, the swags, valance, and dust ruffle are made from the same linen on the armchair in front of the window seat. ABOVE: The mattress-like window seat is upholstered in blue velvet and the armchair in a floral-print linen that looks like faded chintz. The carpet is a mossy trellis pattern with a Maltese cross motif. The brass-trimmed wall lamp is from Galerie des Lampes in Paris.

OPPOSITE: In the master bath, a chinoiserie floral wallpaper surrounds the tub. The antique stool with its original tapestry fabric is the type of offbeat element I like to add to keep a room from seeming too studied. ABOVE: A favorite Rose Tarlow wallpaper was the starting point for a guest bedroom. An exaggerated pagoda valance and lush curtains are a nice counterpoint to the Giacometti-inspired four-poster bed and the sculptural vintage mirror.

CONTEMPORARY GRANDEUR

I f they could, my sister Ophelia and brother-in-law Bill would live at the beach. They adore St. Barts and the Hamptons, but for so many reasons—business, family, friends, culture, civic duty—they must live in New York City, which is their hometown, after all. When they began to look for a new apartment as "empty nesters," their number one priority was outdoor space: They wanted the feeling of a country house in the city, but they were not about to settle for a town house with a small backyard or a penthouse with narrow terraces, so they ended up taking over the entire top floor of a thirty-five-story building in the heart of the Upper East Side. This required a gut renovation of the existing apartments to create one expansive home with two 2,000-square-foot terraces—one facing north and one facing south—that together offer panoramic city views.

I worked closely with the architects Fairfax & Sammons to create a home that would accommodate the unique lifestyle of Ophelia and Bill, along with the needs of my mother who lives with them. (There was also enough room to create a separate apartment for my nephew, who shares one of the terraces with his parents.) Having moved all of their favorite furniture to the family house in the Hamptons, my sister and brother-in-law were starting from scratch with the decorating. Along with a mix of the eighteenth- and twentieth-century furniture and contemporary art that they love, the decor plays off the proximity to the sky with shades of blue in almost every room. Whether entertaining formally or gathering the family together to watch sports or a movie, Ophelia and Bill have a home that offers an elegant embrace.

OPPOSITE: In the foyer, Ophelia wanted Gracie wallpaper with hand-painted peonies and apple blossoms. The contemporary gilded mirror and candlesticks are by Les Lalanne. The Victor Proetz white console with gilt bronze horse-hoof legs is from Louis Bofferding. The chalky-white bench from Jonathan Burden Antiques is upholstered in white horsehair from Clarence House and trimmed with a moss fringe from Samuel & Sons.

RIGHT: For the living room, I designed a new carpet pattern for Beauvais inspired by classic parquet de Versailles. A pair of coffee tables made from eighteenth-century Korean lacquer panels is placed in front of a custom sofa upholstered in Fortuny, which is my sister's favorite fabric. A Jacob chair from Louis Bofferding and a Syrie Maugham chair in tiger-striped silk velvet complete the seating group. The satin curtains and scalloped valance were hand-painted by Andy Holland. The gilded bronze chandelier is Empire.

66

ABOVE: The custom U-shaped sofa upholstered in Fortuny and trimmed in silk velvet works well for cocktail parties or for family TV nights. The Lucite and gilt bronze coffee table is from Maison Jansen. The tree-branch lamp is by John Dickinson from H. M. Luther. The painting is by the abstract artist Jules Olitski. OPPOSITE: A porphyry urn and eighteenth-century German silver tankards are displayed on a stone console, which is in the manner of Emilio Terry and from Glen Dooley Antiques. The white tree-branch painting by Adam Ball is from the Paul Kasmin Gallery.

RIGHT: The dining room expresses my sister's exuberant style with its midnight-blue lacquered walls, vibrant yellow satin curtains, and custom carpet with a pomegranate-and-paisley pattern in coral and blue by Beauvais. The mahogany table from Frederick P. Victoria & Son has gilt bronze mounts and enough leaves to seat twenty people. The eighteenth-century gilt-wood chairs are upholstered in a flame-stitch pattern from Quadrille, and their backs are in a woven silk from Jack Lenor Larsen. The painting is by Julian Schnabel. The beaded chandelier is from Liz O'Brien. The candlesticks are by Marc Bankowsky.

PAGE 72: In my sister's sitting room, the games table from Soane in London has gilt brass legs and a tooled leather top; it is surrounded by chairs from Frederick P. Victoria & Son, which are upholstered on the front in velvet from Scalamandre and on the back in white horsehair from Brunschwig & Fils. The curtains are made from a Cowtan & Tout embroidered silk, and the stenciled floors are by Andy Holland.

OPPOSITE: The sitting room has sunset views, and the afternoon light is magical on the verre églomisé walls with gilded silver-leaf mica dust by Miriam Ellner. A nineteenth-century gilded rope chair from Guinevere Antiques in London is upholstered in satin. The wall sculpture by Anish Kapoor hangs over a vintage steel and bronze console by John Dickinson that holds a wishbone sculpture by Chuck Price.

OPPOSITE: A blue bust by Igor Mitoraj and a pair of Maison Charles brass artichoke lamps grace a desk from Gerald Bland. The gilt Régence chairs are upholstered in an ikat from Carleton V. The satin curtains were hand-stenciled by Andy Holland. ABOVE: The walls of my brother-in-law's office are upholstered in a textured fabric. The custom bookcase has gilt-wood feet and hardware from P. E. Guerin. It is flanked by Maison Jansen chairs with cushions in a woven coral silk.

ABOVE LEFT: Silver faux bois wallpaper from Lee Jofa adds an enchanted atmosphere to a hallway. The torso is by Igor Mitoraj and the lanterns are by Marc Bankowsky. ABOVE RIGHT: The powder room has a vanity designed by Fairfax & Sammons with custom panels by Nancy Lorenz. The gold-plated and patinated apple faucets from P. E. Guerin are a wink to the Big Apple campaign that my brother-in-law's father, Lew, was instrumental in creating. The rocaille gilt-ceramic wall lights are by Eve Kaplan, and the gilt bronze lantern is by Louis Cane. OPPOSITE: My sister's office has lacquer bookcases, a table by Willy Rizzo, and chairs from the Marché aux Puces that we upholstered in metallic leather from Edelman. The rock-crystal chandelier is from Liz O'Brien.

ABOVE: The serene master bedroom has walls upholstered in a white linen basket weave with stenciled strapping by Andy Holland. I designed the bed, which is upholstered in Fortuny and dressed with custom linens from Schweitzer. The bedside tables are by Frederick P. Victoria & Son, and the swing-arm lamps are from Art & Style. The angel rubbing by Igor Mitoraj hangs above the bed.
OPPOSITE: I designed the custom carpet for Beauvais. The gilt-wood settee purchased in New Orleans is paired with an eighteenth-century Japanese lacquer trunk from H. M. Luther and a bronze head by Igor Mitoraj. The curtains are white satin from Lee Jofa with a Samuel & Sons trim.

FIFTH AVENUE SPLENDOR

My clients tend to fully immerse themselves in decorating their homes, which I love because it means we can share the excitement of drawing up plans, considering all the options, and then shopping with a clear sense of mission and passion. The husband and wife who own this airy Fifth Avenue apartment each like different parts of the design process, so I would go to antiques fairs and auction houses with him, and then I would visit designer showrooms with her. They brought different perspectives to the project because he's English and tends to be quite formal, and she's an American with a more casual sensibility. My role was to synthesize their aesthetics to create a home with a layered quality that reflects both their personalities.

While the final result feels perfectly suited for them, it did not happen easily. In fact, we did the scheme four times before we got it just right. The couple has three sons so even though the apartment would be full of fine antiques, it could not be precious or high maintenance. We decided to forgo rugs entirely in the public rooms, and the stenciled designs we chose have a sense of traditional grandeur while being thoroughly modern at the same time. You might think that the overall effect would be austere, but the mood throughout is warm and romantic, with pale colors and plush fabrics providing a mellow counterpoint to the bold antiques. The apartment reflects my belief that even the most sophisticated and elegant home should always feel relaxed and welcoming.

OPPOSITE: Striped wallpaper from Colefax and Fowler and elaborately stenciled floors set the tone in the large entrance foyer. A gilt bronze lantern hangs above an Empire mahogany center table with nineteenth-century gilt hurricanes and an antique globe mounted on eighteenth-century bronze Fu dogs. OVERLEAF: Plain floors with a simple stenciled border are a dignified backdrop for exquisite antiques. One of my favorite pieces is the Baltic secretary that is flanked by French stools upholstered in horsehair in front of the windows. The pillows on the love seat are Fortuny. The marble and gilt bronze coffee table is from New York dealer Louis Bofferding.

OPPOSITE: The sculptural swan-legged Empire chair is upholstered in a yellow-and-white embroidered fabric. The glass-fronted cabinet behind it is Russian. ABOVE: The living room walls are painted a pale yellow and the curtains are a yellow-and-cream damask. The coffee table is by Frederick P. Victoria & Son, who makes furniture that echoes the spirit and craftsmanship of the past. The mahogany Empire chair with the lion's-paw feet is upholstered in a quilted white satin.

ABOVE: The table is set with hand-painted early twentieth-century Bavarian plates and yellow cut-crystal Baccarat goblets. OPPOSITE: The magnificent inlaid dining room table is Italian, and it's paired with Biedermeier chairs with custom-embroidered and appliquéd velvet seats. The walls are upholstered above the chair rail in basket-weave linen. The sconces and chandelier are Empire.

A GALLERY FOR LIVING

There's a new mood on Park Avenue these days, and it's epitomized by these clients who have classic taste when it comes to decorating but an avant-garde sensibility when it comes to collecting art. They wanted their apartment to have the flexibility and airiness of a gallery, so they could rotate their art as new pieces are added to their ever-expanding collection. But they also wanted it to have immutable charm and character—warm, comfortable, and unpretentious—so their children would have a true sense of home.

Furthermore, it had to be drop-dead chic like the incredibly stylish wife, whom I've known since high school. In fact, she's as responsible as anyone for my career. When I was on the cusp of adulthood, she's the one who said to me, "Alex, you have such great taste—you should be a decorator." She even recommended me to her mother, an antiques dealer, who was one of my earliest clients; but when my friend decorated her apartment for the first time she chose an established designer, the legendary Mark Hampton. When her second husband moved in with her, they called me to redo the apartment to make it *their* home. It would have been crazy for them to move, because the apartment is one of New York's best: a full-floor of exquisitely proportioned rooms that had been meticulously renovated with classic architectural flourishes by Ferguson Shamamian & Ratther. My goal was to pare it down and rethink the notion of uptown luxury in a way that would personify my friend's clean elegance and refined sensibility. The husband gave me a crash course in contemporary art, sharing his expertise and passion, which made it an especially exciting project. Because the art, architecture, and antiques were so exquisite, the decorating could be kept rather simple. By using traditional furniture in a modern way so it harmonizes with cutting-edge art, we created a home that is the best of all possible worlds.

OPPOSITE: A painting by Richard Prince and a silver-leaf and rock-crystal chandelier from Liz O'Brien hang above the fireplace in the entrance foyer. The nineteenth-century begère is upholstered in white velvet.

RIGHT: The living room, which is painted Benjamin Moore's Cloud White, is a tone poem in ivory and cream with a mix of textures that make the room warm and inviting. The sofa is upholstered in a linen basket weave with a cotton and silk fringe. The skirted table is covered in a fretwork pattern that's a modern take on lace. One bergère is upholstered in white cotton velvet, and a club chair is in a soft cotton-linen. Pale blue accents contribute to the feeling of tranquility. The carpet is a thick cream-colored basket-weave sisal. The painting over the sofa is by George Condo.

ABOVE: In the living room, an Italian ceramic lamp with a custom silk shade sits on a Giacometti table beside a collection of modern Danish ceramics. The bergère is upholstered in a whisper-soft aqua and trimmed in a gimp. OPPOSITE: A painting by Elizabeth Peyton hangs over an elaborately carved seventeenth-century table. The sculpture of a boy is by the Japanese artist Takashi Murakami.

OPPOSITE: A magnificent eighteenth-century Russian chandelier and a painting by Christopher Wool create a dynamism in the dining room. The table is Regency and so are the chairs, which are upholstered in a pale green horsehair and trimmed in miniature nailheads.
ABOVE: A white sculpture by Rudolf Stingel hangs over a Regency console table.

ABOVE: In the bedroom, a painting by John Currin hangs over an extraordinary *secrétaire à abattant*. The walls are upholstered in a white jacquard, and the curtains are made from a heavy cotton moss-fringed stripe. The nineteenth-century bergère is upholstered in white leather, which gives the chair a modern feel.
OPPOSITE: A photograph by Andreas Gursky hangs on one of the library walls, which are upholstered in a textured basket-weave fabric. The end tables from Maison Bagues flank the sofa upholstered in a camel-colored striae velvet. The lamps are fashioned from old printing forms made of wood and steel. The coffee table was designed by the late Mark Hampton, who decorated the apartment in an earlier iteration.

ABOVE: The family room has a custom tobacco-brown lacquer games table surrounded by Knoll chairs in textured wool on a carpet in my Scott's Chevron pattern from Beauvais. The ikat fabric for the shades is from Holland & Sherry and so is the brown corduroy on the sofa. The custom coffee table is upholstered in glazed linen. The painting over the sofa is by Richard Prince.

OPPOSITE: The breakfast room is glamorous yet practical. The chairs are upholstered in white patent leather, which resists spills. The light fixture is made from spun pieces of Venini glass, and the window shade from a matelassé fabric called Plucked Feathers is from Clarence House.

GENTEEL COUNTRY

There's no one-size-fits-all formula when it comes to country houses, especially when they're more than weekend retreats. My cultured clients in Litchfield County, Connecticut, refused to compromise their elegant standards just because they'd decided to live in a rural community. Although beautifully situated with pastoral views of ponds, fields, and rolling hills, the large house was rather plain, which meant that I needed to apply my entire arsenal—upholstered walls, opulent curtains, custom carpets, and floors—to design a home that would be cozy for two and yet welcoming for the inevitable houseguests.

To establish the impression that you're in a French country house, we built a new sweeping staircase with an ironwork banister (the previous floating one was too contemporary) and installed limestone floors and a limestone mantelpiece in the living room. We collected English, French, and Portuguese antiques, a mix that gives the house a sense of history that reflects the overlapping trade routes of long ago. We layered patterns upon patterns, which creates an exuberant, warm atmosphere. We were exacting about accessories as we always are, making sure that every mirror, lampshade, and sconce contributed to the luxurious, patrician feeling. But what makes this (or any) house sing are the finishing details, and these clients are connoisseurs who will order custom linens or buy a new pair of candlesticks to add another elegant touch to a room. With every purchase and passing year, the house becomes more distinctly their own.

OPPOSITE: A new staircase and limestone floors add drama to the foyer with its original rustic beams. A stunning Regency library table holds a collection of Delft porcelain and Chinese-inspired turned-wood candlesticks from John Rosselli. The chandelier is eighteenth-century Dutch.

ABOVE: One of the seating groups in the living room features a sofa upholstered in a sunny Braquenié and club chairs in an embroidered blue-and-white fabric. The classic coffee table is from Frederick P. Victoria & Son. The Queen Anne console from Hyde Park Antiques serves as a room divider with wooden Venetian lamps that have custom silk lampshades. The elephant garden seat is nineteenth century. OPPOSITE: The foyer has tobacco-leaf wallpaper from Clarence House and a carpet by Stark. The benches from Frederick P. Victoria & Son are upholstered in a Pierre Frey tapestry. The white alabaster lantern is nineteenth century. The owners found the ceramic guard dogs.

RIGHT: A needlepoint rug from one of Portugal's oldest mills adds a rich layer of detail to the living room. The matched pair of antique wing chairs is upholstered in an embroidered check from Pierre Frey, and the sofa is upholstered in a quilted Braquenié. A painted tole basket holds firewood in front of the new limestone mantelpiece.

The terra-cotta figures in the niches are Italian. Instead of one enormous piece of art for the wall, we chose an eighteenth-century country scene in four separate frames. PAGE 106: The dining room walls are upholstered in a Braquenié fabric that I had over-embroidered in India and also used for the seat cushions of the antique Portuguese chairs. The magnificently carved nineteenth-century Anglo-Indian table is from Jonathan Burden in TriBeCa. The brass chandelier is Dutch, and the custom rug was woven in Portugal.

104

OPPOSITE: A guest room has walls upholstered in a Manuel Canovas toile. The bed is upholstered in silk damask and trimmed with a cotton bullion fringe; the bed curtains in a silk stripe. The night table is a burl and gilt bronze guéridon. The chalky-white French chair is upholstered in a green-and-white cut velvet from Old World Weavers. A collection of faience is displayed on the mantel beneath a Georgian convex eagle mirror.

NEW YORK CHIC

Redecorating for longtime clients is as enjoyable as it is inevitable. Once a project is "finished," I am invariably called back to replace some pillows or a chair and hang new art, creating a domino effect that leads to more changes. The owners of this New York town house (who were my friends before they became clients) now have different priorities than when we first gutted and renovated their five-story home some twenty years ago. Back then, they wanted the house to be modern and super glamorous, but I insisted on classic plaster moldings and a bronze scrolled staircase that would stand the test of time. I love the juxtaposition of classic architecture and modern decoration because it's ageless. If everything's too modern, it begins to look like a hip hotel (if you know what I mean), and it quickly becomes dated.

Since the couple has four children, I have been tweaking the kids' rooms as they've grown and I've become close to the entire family. Meanwhile, the parents started acquiring contemporary art, and they asked me to update the rooms to be a better backdrop for their growing collection. In their earlier days, they had liked shiny, shimmery surfaces, but now they wanted everything to be more relaxed and cozy while still unabashedly modern.

They were becoming more casual, too, and they were willing to forgo their formal dining room to create a family room where everyone could hang out. Now they watch television, share family meals, and host dinner parties in the same expansive, tailored space. It suits their personalities and their entertaining style, which often brings together several generations simultaneously. Houses, like people, must evolve to stay relevant, and this house continues to be interesting and vital, well used and well loved.

OPPOSITE: I designed a pedestal out of antique mirrors for the sculpture in the foyer. The staircase has a swank wool zebra-print rug that wears like iron, which is essential in a house with four children. The poured- and mirrored-glass artwork that runs along the staircase is by Rob Wynne. OVERLEAF: Even with its original ornate moldings, the living room feels modern, with its gray silk wallpaper, white mohair sofas, a custom contemporary coffee table in shagreen and bronze, and an abstract painting by Shirazeh Houshiary.

ABOVE (CLOCKWISE FROM TOP LEFT): An antique deity looks at home on a pedestal reflecting a geometric-stenciled floor by Andy Holland; a steel and gilt bronze chest is the basis for a vignette that includes a black patent leather chair, a painting by Callum Innes, and a gilt fly-on-the-wall by Rob Wynne; the powder room, which is tucked under the staircase, has a sink fashioned from an antique jardiniere; a vintage Tommi Parzinger console is paired with a gilt and white-painted mirror.

OPPOSITE: The old mantel was too traditional for the updated decor, so I designed a new one in steel and brass that's substantial and chic. The three-dimensional mirrored collage is by Dmitri Plavinsky.

LEFT: In the living room, the clear
piano by Kawai is a showstopper.
The vintage bench by Karl Springer
is upholstered in a silk animal print
from Schumacher. The window seat
has silk velvet cushions and silk
taffeta shades; the sisal carpet is
from Beauvais. The teardrops on the
wall are by Rob Wynne. The bunny
sculpture is by Alexander Kosolapov.

119

ABOVE AND OPPOSITE: In the family room, the square dining table, the Christian Liaigre–style chairs, and the bronze and glass chandelier with a silk shade were all custom-designed. The walls are covered in grass paper above and below the chair rail. The Warhol silk screen of Richard Nixon adds a major pop of color, as does the photo weaving by Dinh Q. Lê. One sofa is upholstered in quilted cotton and the other in a cut velvet. The pillows are in assorted fabrics, including a pattern by Allegra Hicks. The Coromandel screen is an unexpected but charming Old World element.

PHOTOGRAPHS
1961-1967

DEN
H

ABOVE: The master bedroom is a plush cocoon with a brown suede sleigh bed and wool sateen upholstered walls. The white satin curtains on a nickel and brass pole have custom-made square pulls and rings with matchstick blinds beneath. The bedside tables and lamps are from two of my favorite sources, Frederick P. Victoria & Son and Christopher Spitzmiller, respectively. The geometric carpet adds a layer of pizzazz.

OPPOSITE: The wife's dressing room is her personal haven and reflects her European fashion sense. It has cream-colored patent leather walls, a leopard-print carpet, custom mirrored chests, and a black Venetian glass chandelier. A sexy black patent leather chair is paired with a modern bronze desk.

OLD WORLD OPULENCE

My family's beach house is admittedly more cosmopolitan and opulent than your typical country house, but it's a clear reflection of who we are: the most informal formal people you could ever meet. We have four generations (and five dogs) living together on weekends all year long, and it's where we celebrate Thanksgiving and Christmas—a true family home. My sister Ophelia has been my greatest champion and client from the very beginning, so to share a house with her is a true blessing. Most of the antiques here once graced the Manhattan apartments of my mother and my sister, so the furniture is familiar to us and imbued with wonderful memories. We did not even reupholster the sofas with their over-embroidery from my sister's Park Avenue living room, and they look divine in the country setting. Although the house, which is set on five acres, is quite large, it has a cozy feel: All the fabrics are soft, lush, textured, and dog friendly.

Everything's been thought out to suit our lives because we've done several major renovations with the remarkable architect Kitty McCoy. We built a new TV room with a custom sofa that can seat twelve, because we love to watch movies *en famille*. The tables in the dining room and breakfast room can be expanded with leaves so that houseguests always feel welcome. The games table in the living room is where we play *biriba*, a Greek card game that has become an obsession, which means that our living room is rarely empty. I'm a firm believer that living rooms should be used daily and not reserved for company. Whether we're in our bathing suits or dressed up for a cocktail party, the house is always accommodating. Of course, everyone has a sumptuous bedroom where they can find some peace and quiet if that is what they need. By surrounding ourselves with the people and things that we love, we gain a sense of joy and well-being, so we return to the city on Sunday nights rejuvenated.

OPPOSITE: The entry foyer, which has wallpaper with an acorn-and-bamboo motif, has a pair of eighteenth-century walnut and gilt-wood Italian mirrors over English Regency consoles. The neoclassical candlesticks are gilt bronze and marble, and the covered pot is nineteenth-century Chinese.

ABOVE: Originally a builder's spec house, we've made many changes to put our stamp on the property. The driveway was relandscaped to showcase a provocative white cast-steel tree sculpture by Ugo Rondinone. OPPOSITE: The fabric-covered hall table with its dense wool trim is a warm counterpoint to a stenciled floor that's my variation of those found in Russian palaces.

RIGHT: Set on bare floors, the extravagant over-embroidered sofas from my sister's apartment in the city take on a more casual air. Trimmed in nailheads instead of gimp, the gilt French Régence chair is upholstered in a gaufrage bouclé. The coffee table is gilt bronze, and the painting over the fireplace is by Charles Arnoldi.

ANTHONY VAN DYCK

ABOVE: The third matching sofa is flanked by a pair of French gilt-wood chairs that are upholstered in a silk velvet leopard print; they're big, comfy, and sturdy, which makes them perfect for the country. The photograph above the sofa is by Mona Kuhn. The gilt fluted coffee table has a mirrored top and shelf. The whimsical turtle footstool is similar to one owned by the late Sunny von Bülow.
OPPOSITE: Formal furniture feels more relaxed with countrified fabrics, such as the Regency chairs upholstered in a reverse chintz and a linen print. Instead of having curtains on every window in the living room, a single metropolitan shade with a velvet welt was used in two corners.

ABOVE, (CLOCKWISE FROM TOP LEFT): I love the juxtaposition of Japanese presentation baskets with antique silk cords and a nineteenth-century console and a gilt-wood mirror; the essential games table was made by Frederick P. Victoria & Son and the chalky-white chairs are upholstered in Fortuny; a mixed-media work by Claes Oldenburg hangs over an architect's desk that's used here as a bookcase; a gilt bronze and mirrored inkstand shares a tabletop with a tiger's-eye box and marble urns. OPPOSITE: The Regency desk behind the sofa was one of my sister's favorite pieces from her New York apartment. The silk lampshade with a silk gimp casts a warm glow over assorted objets d'art.

132

RIGHT: We decided to treat the space between the living and dining rooms as a sunroom, with walls covered in a floral print from Cowtan & Tout. The daybeds by Bielecky Brothers—wonderful for napping in the afternoon or group chats during a party—have cushions made from a Clarence House linen. The chalky-white armchair is upholstered in a velvet flame-stitch pattern. The eighteenth-century grisailles on the walls used to be in my mother's Manhattan living room. OVERLEAF: A Russian-inspired neoclassical bookcase with brass inlays was custom-made by Frederick P. Victoria & Son; formerly the TV cabinet in my sister's library in the city, we put it in the dining room, where it now holds a collection of antique books. Holland & Sherry did the magnificent silk and mohair embroidery on the wool sateen chairs, which have brass inlays. The French table has no apron but many leaves, making it very flexible. The walls are covered in a favorite faux bois paper that has the texture of real wood.

ABOVE (CLOCKWISE FROM TOP LEFT): In the dining room, an oversize hurricane originally made by Frederick P. Victoria & Son for the Duke and Duchess of Windsor; a gilt bronze telescope table in the TV room; the powder room sink is fashioned out of an antique jardiniere and paired with gilt-wood Adams sconces and a Regency mirror; the powder room walls are covered in a printed grass cloth, and the bronze figure is based on Michelangelo's slave sculptures. OPPOSITE: Teddy, one of our household's five dogs, poses in front of a bust of Homer on a pedestal with a speckled finish in the TV room. The neoclassical Russian chairs are upholstered in Fortuny.

138

PRECEDING SPREAD: The U-shaped sofa upholstered in a Fortuny cotton can seat twelve people for watching movies. The coffee tables were designed as ottomans so you can put up your feet. The walls are upholstered in lush velvet and the carpet has the look of moire. The nineteenth-century French gilt-wood stools are upholstered in Fortuny as well. RIGHT: We hung an enormous Venetian chandelier over the indoor pool, which is slightly crazy but incredibly divine. The curtains and upholstery are made from an all-weather fabric. The bronze sconces from Maison Gerard are by the French artist Marc Bankowsky.

ABOVE: Sebastian stands guard in the kitchen designed by architect Kitty McCoy and painted in Benjamin Moore's Ivory White. The hardware is nickel plated. OPPOSITE: The table in the breakfast room has leaves because we often have ten or twelve people for breakfast when we have houseguests. The chairs have Colefax and Fowler seats that are laminated so that they can be easily wiped clean. The stenciled floors and oversize lantern are in keeping with the mood of the rest of the house. OVERLEAF: The Regency chair is upholstered in gaufrage velvet, and the eighteenth-century French commode is from Todd Romano. I created the custom bed with lion's-paw feet for my own bedroom, which has striae wallpaper from Cowtan & Tout. The pillows and curtains are made from a Bennison fabric with yellow birds. I never draw the curtains, which have a taffeta lining and silk velvet trim; I merely pull down the blackout matchstick blinds. The bedside tables are French lacquer with stone tops.

ABOVE: Friends always request a stay in this guest room with its divine leafy wallpaper from Cowtan & Tout. The chinoiserie commode is from John Rosselli. OPPOSITE: An ebonized four-poster bed from Robert Lighton is dressed in an over-embroidered fabric from Clarence House. An antique quilt in perfect condition is paired with custom-trimmed sheets. I had the vintage palm-tree lamps painted chalky white to make them more romantic.

RIGHT: I designed this enormous sleigh bed in silk velvet for the master bedroom after seeing pictures of the incomparable Marie Hélène de Rothschild's bedroom. The contemporary silk and gilt-wood discs by artist Justen Ladda on the aqua walls are a graphic counterpoint to the old-fashioned silk taffeta curtains that have the glamour of a ball gown. The bench at the foot of the bed came from my mother's country house, and I had it painted chalky white.

LEONARDO DA VINCI

The Ultimate Rose Book

Armand Hammer Collection

ABOVE: The pool house chairs are based on an antique that I found in the Paris flea market. They are perfectly scaled—what I call a "big little chair"—and now I often reproduce them for clients. Here, they're upholstered in a plaid from Lee Jofa. The sofa is covered in an all-weather gaufrage velvet, and the pillows are made from a vintage bird-and-floral fabric that Lee Jofa recolored to my specifications for a Southampton show house; the combination of gray, white, and blue gave the fabric a modern personality. The standing lamps are nickel plated. OPPOSITE: On the porch, where we have drinks in the summer, the custom Bielecky Brothers wicker seating has cushions made from a vintage Billy Baldwin print reproduced by Quadrille.

ABOVE: My sister's father-in-law was one of the civic leaders who popularized the nicknaming of New York as the "Big Apple," so she was so excited when she saw this gigantic apple by Les Lalanne; we positioned it in the garden so it looks as if it might have just fallen off a nearby tree. OPPOSITE: The family made a pilgrimage to the studio of the Polish artist Igor Mitoraj in Tuscany, where my sister chose this surreal and monumental sculpture for the garden.

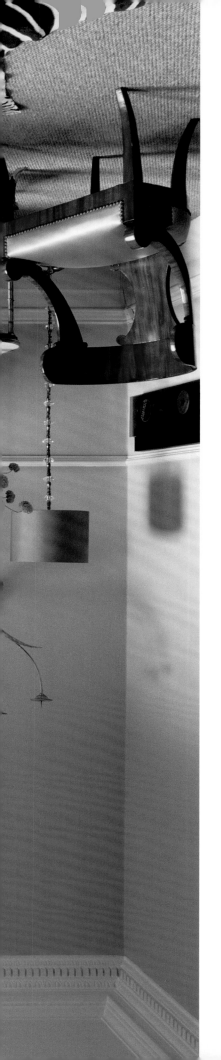

EUROPEAN COUTURE

I'm invariably attracted to people with strong points of view, such as my jewelry designer friend, who used to be my decorating colleague. Glamour is an essential aspect of her personality, which is evident from the types of antiques she collects and the clothes she wears, but simplicity is just as important to her. Although she is very elegant and ladylike, she is drawn to furniture that has a bold, muscular quality. Her apartments have a blend of masculine and feminine elements that fit her like a haute couture gown, a precisely tailored expression of her personal style.

Our first collaboration was her flat in London (which appeared on the cover of *Elle Decor*), and she made it clear that she envisioned it as restrained but recherché. She wanted a soothing, soft gray envelope and allowed me to add a few dashes of color and pattern that would augment the intrepid collection of furniture and art we were amassing. Because she is drawn to the neoclassical, we could mix eighteenth-, nineteenth-, and twentieth-century pieces that would all relate to one another. The effect is fastidious and fresh—a pared-down opulence that's breathtaking and intoxicating.

RIGHT: A pair of Italian gilt-wood sconces flank a collection of nineteenth-century drawings hung in a graphic grid on pale gray walls. The custom velvet sofa by Soane has silk trim and gilt finials and lion's-paw feet. The neoclassical chairs are Russian and the coffee table is gilt bronze with a lacquer top by Maison Baguès. A zebra-skin rug laid over the sisal carpet is a sassy touch.

ABOVE: A nineteenth-century Italian chaise longue has a neoclassical profile. It's upholstered in gray-and-white-striped silk taffeta. The standing gilt bronze lamp from Maison Baques has a gray silk shade that's in keeping with the room's subdued palette. The eighteenth-century *secrétaire à abattant* in the adjoining room belonged to the owner's grandmother. OPPOSITE: The entry foyer can double as a dining room. The 1970s steel and glass table is paired with nineteenth-century Italian ebonized and gilt chairs. The Venetian chandelier was bought at the Paris flea market. The black-and-white photographs included a portrait of the owner taken by a friend. The color photographs are by Luis González Palma, who's represented by London dealer Patrizia Papachristidis of E. B. & Flow.

158

ABOVE: In the guest room, sculptural lamps with amethyst silk shades sit on a 1940s brass and lacquer desk by Maison Jansen. The brass side chairs, which came from an old train, have plum velvet upholstery. The Victorian gilt-wood chair is upholstered in Fortuny. OPPOSITE: The walls are burlap, and the nineteenth-century French painted daybed has gray satin cushions. The curtains are made of a plum silk jacquard from the Silk Trading Company. The ram's-head light fixture is from Mrs. MacDougall.

COUTURE CLASSIC

When my friend decided to move back to New York City from London, we had the unique opportunity to edit her collection, and it's interesting how the smaller scale of the Manhattan apartment affected how we saw things. The Russian chairs and drawings from the London living room are now in the New York foyer. The large neoclassical mirrors that were in her London bedroom are now in her living room, along with the sconces that seemed rather demure in London yet now make a big statement. Once again, she wanted gray walls, which seemed fresh here because the light in New York is so different than in London. The rooms are a pure, icy gray that feels incredibly luxurious and modern.

While we repurposed many pieces—the lamps from the London guest room are now on her bedside tables with new shades—the scale of the apartment required some serious editing. The Venetian chandelier had to be sold because it was just too large for the new place. There wasn't room for the daybed, but she decided to put it in storage because she couldn't bear to part with it. She didn't want anything fussy, which is why we did not use carpets but instead did a graphic stenciled floor throughout (which I'd originally done to great effect for my mother's apartment many years ago). She doesn't like a lot of upholstery either, but I did design two new pieces for her: a sofa and a bed that are both covered in a chic gray satin.

OPPOSITE: The nineteenth-century drawings and neoclassical Russian chairs from the London flat reappear in the foyer of the New York apartment along with a newly purchased Art Deco table and a mid-century chandelier with pierced brass shades that hang from silk cords. The floors throughout are stenciled in a bold graphic pattern that makes the small apartment seem larger.

ABOVE: A French nineteenth-century commode with marquetry and a marble top is paired with a contemporary collage and one of Frederick P. Victoria & Son's oversized hurricanes. OPPOSITE: Large-scale objects add grandeur to a small space, and the nineteenth-century mirror hung close to the ceiling looks smart with the neoclassical chaise and gilt-wood sconces. Gilt x-frame benches are paired with a burl marquetry table with ivory feet. OVERLEAF: I designed the winged sofa after one from Maison Jansen. We modernized it with a mattress sofa cushion in gray satin and gilt-wood bun feet. The gilt bronze tree-branch coffee table with a lacquer top is by Maison Bagues. The *secrétaire à abattant* holds a vintage Venetian glass lamp. The stacks of books on the floor have a counterintuitive chic.

ABOVE: Two eighteenth-century candlesticks that have been turned into *bouillotte* lamps stand atop a Biedermeier commode. OPPOSITE: I designed the satin upholstered bed as well as the sheets. The lamps from her previous apartment have new gray silk shades. The bedside tables are mirrored brass by Maison Bagues.

168

ELEGANT PIED-À-TERRE

Passionate about collecting art, these European clients are equally serious about interior design. Many years ago, they worked with the legendary English decorator David Hicks, and they have a keen understanding of antiques and a profound appreciation for the craftsmanship required to create a beautiful home. When they decided to buy a pied-à-terre in New York City, they wanted to renovate, decorate, and move in as quickly as possible. They had great expectations that I could transform their quotidian postwar Fifth Avenue apartment into an impeccable prewar-style home. It was exactly the type of challenge I love: providing an Old World flavor where there isn't any. I worked with New York architect Alan Orenbuch, who understands how to create a classic backdrop for contemporary life with just the right balance of moldings and paneling, so it's as if you've stepped into a well-preserved residence with an updated, modern feel.

To provide a focal point for the living room and evoke a sense of prewar charm, there's a faux fireplace and mantel, but everything else in the apartment is either a fine antique or a custom-made piece that I designed specifically for this project. To set a classical atmosphere, we installed parquet de Versailles, chose a color palette that suggests eternal spring, and shopped for French antiques that would complement the impressive paintings and exquisite porcelains they would be bringing to their new home. It's inspiring to see how they care for the apartment by filling the rooms with fresh flowers when they're in residence and making sure that everything's immaculate. I appreciate clients who understand that living well is an art form unto itself.

OPPOSITE: In the entrance hall, a lithograph by Jean Dubuffet hangs over an eighteenth-century French commode with a marble top and a stunning collection of Asian artifacts: a fifteenth-century copper alloy Buddha from Thailand; two eighteenth-century Tibetan monks in gilt copper; a Chinese Tang Dynasty Sancai glazed Guan jar; and a Chinese Han Dynasty green glazed stoneware jar.

RIGHT: With walls upholstered in a camel-hued silk satin, the apartment is dressy and elegant. The custom Jansen-inspired sofa in camel silk velvet has a gilt-wood base, and the eighteenth-century chairs flanking it are upholstered in a faux bois fabric. The curtains are made from a printed silk damask and hung on a gilt-wood and mahogany rod. The coffee table is by Giacometti, and the custom side tables were made by Frederick P. Victoria & Son. The eighteenth-century jars mounted as lamps have shades made from a small silk check by Colefax and Fowler. The camel-colored wool carpet is Mughal Lattice by Beauvais.

172

OPPOSITE: The eighteenth-century French fruitwood armless chairs are covered in a hand-blocked chintz that looks like a watercolor, and all the colors in the room—aqua, camel, green, and white—emanate from that fabric. The clients found the antique French sconces themselves on 1stdibs. The painting over the mantel is by Odilon Redon. ABOVE: The "Givenchy" sofa, as it's known in my office, is upholstered in a plush green striae velvet from Colefax and Fowler and trimmed in woven silk tape. The fruitwood stools are covered in a geometric chevron weave from Claremont that lends a modern touch. The big neoclassical chair is one of those hard-to-find antique furnishings in which a man can actually sit comfortably; it is upholstered in cut velvet. The painting over the sofa is by Hans Hofmann. The painting behind the chair is by Sean Scully, and the torso is tenth-century Cambodian.

ABOVE: The dining room is upholstered in a smoky-gray wool sateen above the chair rail. A collection of silver is displayed on a marble-topped French Empire sideboard. The white plaster Serge Roche sconces pick up the white in the chairs. The diptych is by Sean Scully. OPPOSITE: The chalky-white dining room chairs are covered in a woven bouclé that resembles needlepoint. The mahogany table is French nineteenth century and the chandelier is French eighteenth century. I designed the velvet bookcase trimmed in French nailheads to showcase the owners' collection of porcelain.

RIGHT: Raffia wallpaper from Clarence House adds a layer of warmth to his dressing room that has the feel of a library. The sofa and shade are made from a Charlotte Moss fabric by Brunschwig & Fils. A pair of French chairs is upholstered in two fabrics: the front is in a linen-cotton leopard print and the back in a green stripe. The coffee table is of parchment and brass, and the swing-arm lamps are from Galerie des Lampes in Paris. The painting is by Roger Bissière.

ABOVE: A wonderfully evocative gray-blue chintz from Warner of London was used for the headboard, the bed skirt trimmed in a woven wool tape, and the curtains trimmed in wool fringe. The chalky-white and green bed was custom-made by Frederick P. Victoria & Son. The antique bench is upholstered in horsehair.
OPPOSITE: We arranged the owners' collection of porcelain on gilt brackets hung on walls covered in a striae wallpaper from Cowtan & Tout. A French Régence chair upholstered in a dazzling flame-stitch velvet is paired with a Régence desk. The gilt bronze standing lamps are from Mrs. MacDougall.

BEACH BOHEMIAN

As much as I like flights of fancy, I believe that good decorating is all about what's appropriate. You have to take into account geography, climate, and culture. When New York City clients told me they'd purchased a beach house in Provincetown on Cape Cod, I immediately understood that they'd been drawn to this old fishing village because it's a casual, unpretentious place with a bohemian history. They wanted their house to be unmistakably chic but contextual, too; they didn't want to make a big decorating statement. The house needed to have a mellow, barefoot-in-the-dunes ambience so it would be in sync with the community.

It also had to be super comfortable and effortlessly organized so the clients could kick back and enjoy their vacation time (although they knew themselves well enough to ask that I design a home office where they could work separately and together). The house was brand-new, and they wanted everything ready as quickly as possible, so I tried to limit the number of special-order items. Nevertheless, I opted for a custom carpet in the living room—a low-key Indian trellis pattern that pulls everything together. And once I decided to custom-order the rug for the master bedroom as well, I couldn't resist having fabric custom-printed in India for the bed and the curtains, too.

But I also shopped retail, which is not the norm for me. The house was a great opportunity to use John Robshaw's soulful, hand-blocked prints and batiks, which I have long admired. They're wonderful for a beach house—especially in indigo—but there's nothing clichéd about them. By tweaking convention while respecting tradition, we created a free-spirited but tailored retreat.

OPPOSITE: In the khaki-green foyer, a graphic mirror and contemporary nickel sconces hang over a midcentury American chest with woven-rope doors.

182

PRECEDING SPREAD: A custom blue-and-café-au-lait wool rug woven in India sets the attitude in the airy living room. The matching custom sofas are upholstered in a sturdy mattress ticking, and the armchairs in a jaunty batik from John Robshaw. A white tree-branch end table is a sharp contrast to the dark custom coffee table made of reclaimed wood. The windows are deliberately bare to make the most of the view. ABOVE: The newly built house has enviable views of the bay. OPPOSITE: A games table is essential in the living room of any vacation house. This lacquered version is surrounded by wicker chairs upholstered in a John Robshaw fabric.

ABOVE: A stained oak bar from Mrs. MacDougall is the base for a striking vignette with two white tree-branch lamps from Vaughan and a three-dimensional collage that reminds me of the boxes of Joseph Cornell. OPPOSITE: I hung a mid-century white plastic light as if it were a piece of sculpture over a vintage Danish bar.

RIGHT: In the dining room, an oval marble-topped Saarinen table is surrounded by Danish chairs upholstered in vintage silk from John Robshaw. The chandelier is new, but it has the eccentricity of a flea-market find. On the back wall, a vintage mahogany room divider adds a strong architectural presence. The window shades were made from a John Robshaw cotton.

ABOVE: The bed is upholstered in a custom brown-and-white flame-stitch cotton fabric that I had hand-printed in India and also used for the shades and curtains. I found the Anglo-Indian bench at John Robshaw's showroom.
OPPOSITE: The vintage Danish chair and ottoman are upholstered in another John Robshaw fabric. The custom carpet is a companion to the one in the living room.

ABOVE: The twin guest beds are upholstered in chocolate-brown linen, which I also used for the shades. The quilts and carpet are from John Robshaw. The photographs of shells were purchased at Christie's. OPPOSITE: The glass-topped dresser was designed to fit precisely between the two windows; it's upholstered in navy linen and trimmed in silver nailheads.

LIKE A MOTH TO A FLAME

FRENCH RIVIERA   ASSOULINE

Nan Goldin
I'LL BE YOUR MIRROR

LAYERED LUXURY

I lived in the apartment for twenty-three ye
and it exemplifies my belief that good decorating is enduring and timeless. It's important to cr
a backdrop that evolves as you collect paintings, books, and decorative objects, allowing yo
expand your world even if you stay in the same place. Certainly, my apartment adapted a decade
when my partner, Scott Nelson, moved in with me. Initially, he did not fully comprehend my m
is-more philosophy and wondered why we had to live with so much stuff. But, slowly, he bega
understand how much I am engaged and energized by the things that surround us. Eventu
Scott came around, and one night after a party at a very sleek but minimally decorated apartn
he said to me, "That house was so cold and austere. I don't know how people live that way."
been seduced by living in rooms that are plush, layered, and dense with color. Now he ca
imagine living any other way.

Although it was just a one-bedroom apartment with a library, our home felt expansive in
sense. We always found space for the purchases we made on our travels, and we could al
accommodate extra guests when we entertained, because at last count there were twenty-six p
to sit in the living/dining room. It was a happy home and, fortunately, we were able to take al
beloved possessions with us when we moved to our new apartment.

OPPOSITE: The two-sided chinoiserie bookcase was an impulse purchase
while shopping with a friend in Hudson, New York. I told her I thought it w
chicest thing I'd ever seen, and she said, "Where on earth are you going to
I said, "I'll figure it out," and I popped it between the dining and living roor
it became a showstopper. When you fall in love with something, you make it

196

RIGHT: The sofa is upholstered in six different fabrics—including two Bennison prints, a silk velvet, a cut velvet, and a tapestry—for a look that feels casual but was, in fact, methodically planned. The nineteenth-century gilt chairs are covered in Fortuny and the backs in a Scalamandre silk stripe. The armchair is upholstered in a silk faille ikat from Travers. The top of the custom gilt-bamboo coffee table from John Rosselli was painted to resemble Delft tiles. A pair of gilded tole lanterns that hold candles flank a painting of a blackamoor by Rob Wynne. A pair of gueridons that belonged to my mother hold lamps from John Rosselli with chintz shades trimmed in fringe. The gilt turtle footstool is similar to one owned by Sunny von Bülow; I loved it so much that I bought an identical one for my sister.

198

OPPOSITE: The bed is upholstered in gaufrage velvet, and the colorful pillows are made from a Claremont ikat. The bedside tables are from Slatkin & Co., and the Christopher Spitzmiller lamps have shades in a Pierre Frey floral. ABOVE: The bamboo wallpaper in the bedroom pays homage to Billy Baldwin. I love how mod it looks with the Pop Beatles prints by Richard Avedon. The desk is eighteenth-century French, and the bergère is covered in vintage Fortuny that I used on the reverse for an antique look.

A SOPHISTICATED PALETTE

I had no intention of moving until my sister and brother-in-law found the perfect new home in the heart of the Upper East Side. The lure of living in the same building with them and my mother (as well as my nieces and nephew, who have their own apartments at the same address) was irresistible. And so was the prospect of a three-bedroom corner apartment on a high floor with a formal dining room, a library, and spectacular city views.

Scott was as excited as I was by the prospect of more space. We are collectors, and our apartment was overflowing. After living together for eleven years, our tastes are pretty much in sync, so he trusted me on every decision, although he had some very definite ideas about his dressing room, which is a Louis Philippe–style fabric cocoon with concealed closets and a desk with stunning westerly views. (He also has his own bathroom with a tub, while I have one with a stall shower.) We had to renovate, of course, which gave me the opportunity to indulge a few of my fantasies, so now I have a luggage closet, a hall of well-lit cabinets for my large china collection, and my dog, Teddy, who is paper-trained has his own discrete mirrored-and-paneled alcove.

The apartment explodes with pattern and color, an ebullient contrast to the grays and browns that define the streets of New York. The fanciful tented foyer was inspired by the twentieth-century French decorator Georges Geffroy, who worked for many of Europe's grande dames and great hostesses.

OPPOSITE: The double-sided chinoiserie bookcase takes center stage in the whimsically tented foyer. The walls and mitered ceiling are covered in an exuberant Oscar de la Renta striped fabric. The antique chandelier is tole and gilt with painted flowers and leaves. The stenciled floor was inspired by an André Arbus carpet.

RIGHT: In the living room, Andy Holland outdid himself with the stenciled parquet de Versailles floors. The plum satin valance and swags have braided trim in Prussian blue. The lamps that I designed for Christopher Spitzmiller sit on my mother's gueridons, which flank the sofa upholstered in a cut velvet from Fortuny. The coffee table that I found at William Doyle Galleries has the spirit of a piece by Maison Jansen, and the gilt rope stool is Louis Philippe. The upholstered armchair is one I found in Paris many years ago; it's the perfect "big little chair"; I often have it reproduced for clients, but this is the original. The Chinese bamboo chair was deliberately chosen for contrast and to tone down the room.

OPPOSITE: A French gilt-metal-strapped chest of drawers with bronzed lion's-paw feet is paired with side chairs upholstered in two contrasting satins. The cloisonné figure of a man on a deer is nineteenth century. ABOVE: The scenic chinoiserie wallpaper is based on an eighteenth-century document that I saved for a long time. I gave the document to Gracie, the renowned wallpaper company, which produced a hand-painted paper in shades of brown, green, gold, and Prussian blue. The custom plum-velvet sofa has embroidered Donghia pillows. The gilt armchairs have Claremont patterned cushions and antique ikat backs. The coffee table is gilt faux bois, and the camel table is one of those nineteenth-century wonders that collapses so you can travel with it.

Geffroy was known for adding tiger-print velvet pillows in otherwise classical rooms. I always wanted a tented room inspired by the one he designed for Arturo Lopez-Willshaw's yacht. I think of it as being very Parisian, very chic. The idea for using such an intense and richly detailed chinoiserie wallpaper in the living room came from my memory of Jayne Wrightsman's Palm Beach house by Denning & Fourcade, which had previously been owned by Mona Williams and decorated by Syrie Maugham. A boldly patterned dining room is not uncommon, but a living room like hers—and ours—you don't quickly forget.

I brought most of the furniture from our previous apartment, reupholstering many pieces that, with different fabrics, now look brand-new while maintaining their cozy familiarity. Every room is treated like a jewel box, with shiny objects glimmering and competing for your attention. I've discovered that the lush colors make people happy—the rooms possess a joie de vivre that is contagious. When friends come over for drinks before we head to a restaurant, they usually say, "Why are we going out? Can't we just stay *here*?" They find the opulence dazzling and beguiling.

Moving in was easy because I had planned the installation like a military maneuver—everything had its place. The biggest challenge was unpacking and organizing the 200 boxes of books. The apartment is decorated within an inch of its life, but we can live no other way. We have made a home that is unmistakably and irrepressibly us.

OPPOSITE: The dining room is a tone poem in shades of plum with wool felt walls and satin curtains. The custom laquered table is surrounded by chalky-white chairs upholstered in Fortuny. The nineteenth-century tole chandelier is from John Rosselli. The glass peace sign by Rob Wynne was a Christmas gift I gave to Scott. The shell-encrusted bust presides over meals, as it did in our previous apartment. The stenciled floors are rectangles with squares on the diagonal.

RIGHT: For the library, my Beauvais carpet pattern known as Scott's Chevron was custom-colored in two shades of red and brown. The walls are upholstered in deep plum cotton velvet. The sofa is a mélange of six different fabrics. The chalky-green Syrie Maugham chairs that flank the gilt-bamboo coffee table from John Rosselli are upholstered in Fortuny. The Christopher Spitzmiller lamps have shades made from a cut-up piece of batik. The custom Parsons bookshelves are upholstered in wool felt from Cowtan & Tout. A pair of Chinese yellow Fu dogs are displayed on gilt-wood brackets carved with three feathers, which is the crest of the Prince of Wales that was used by the Duke of Windsor; they flank a painting from our previous apartment by Rob Wynne. The pagoda lantern was custom-painted by Paul Boyko to match the room.

RIGHT: In the master bedroom, I chose a Swedish wallpaper from Old World Weavers, which reminds me of Charles de Beistegui's *Château de Groussay*. I paired it with other strong patterns—a batik bedspread and Beauvais' Mariya trellis carpet, which is named for my mother. The custom velvet bed has cheeky lion's-paw feet. A pair of cut-velvet green pillows perches on top of the custom Matouk linens. The chalky-white chair reupholstered in Fortuny was my mother's, and the little white chair with leopard-print upholstery is for our dog, Teddy, so that he can jump on the bed. The sunburst mirror is 1950s French.

216

ABOVE: Scott's dressing room is an old-fashioned gentleman's sitting room and his personal haven. The walls of concealed closets are upholstered in a tree-of-life-inspired fabric from Manuel Canovas. The geometric carpet is my design for Beauvais. The daybed is topped by a coronet lined in raspberry silk satin. OPPOSITE: The armoire with Coromandel panels is from our previous apartment, and so is the chair. The Venetian blackamoor sconces have Fortuny lampshades.

DESIGN RESOURCES

MADE TO MEASURE

Alan Orenbuch, Architect
1 Union Square West, Suite 814
New York, New York 10003
212.633.3600
www.orenbucharchitect.com

Beauvais Carpets
595 Madison Avenue, 3rd Floor
New York, New York 10022
212.688.2229
www.beauvaiscarpets.com

Bielecky Brothers Inc.
979 Third Avenue, Suite 911
New York, New York 10022
212.753.2355
www.bieleckybrothers.com

Blanche P. Field
155 East 56th Street
New York, New York 10022
212.355.6616
www.blanchefield.com

Charles H. Beckley, Inc.
979 Third Avenue, Suite 911
New York, New York 10022
212.759.8450
www.chbeckley.com

David Monn, LLC Designer
135 West 27th Street, Suite 2
New York, New York 10001
212.242.2009
www.davidmonn.com

Extraordinary Furniture
4301 21st Street, Suite 219
Long Island City, New York 11101
718.786.5204

Fairfax & Sammons Architects
67 Gansevoort Street, 2nd Floor
New York, New York 10014
212.255.0704
www.fairfaxandsammons.com

Frederick P. Victoria & Son, Inc.
21-07 Borden Avenue, 3rd Floor
Long Island City, New York 11102
718.392.9651
www.fpvictoria.com

Gracie, Inc.
979 Third Avenue, Suite 1411
New York, New York 10022
212.924.6816
www.graciestudio.com

Holland & Sherry
979 Third Avenue, Suite 1402
New York, New York 10022
212.355.6241
www.hollandandsherry.com

Jose Quintana Upholstery
43-02 22nd Street, Suite 115
Long Island City, New York 11101
718.361.0946

Kathrine McCoy, Architect LLC
P.O. Box 1557
Bridgehampton, New York 11932
631.537.7588
www.kmccoyarchitect.com

Langhorne Carpet Company
201 West Lincoln Highway
Penndel, Pennsylvania 19047
215.757.5155
www.langhornecarpets.com

New York Drapery Inc.
147 West 25th Street, 7th Floor
New York, New York 10001
212.229.1533

Optical Grays Inc.
300 East 93rd Street, Suite 40A
New York, New York 10128
212.686.7371

Paul Boyko Inc.
320 East 95th Street
New York, New York 10128
212.410.0614

Schweitzer Linen
1053 Lexington Avenue
New York, New York 10021
212.570.0236
www.schweitzerlinen.com

Vera Iachia
Portuguese Needle Rugs
Rua das Flores 105
1200 Lisbon, Portugal
+351.21.387.33.71
www.veraiachia.com

Wadia Associates
134 Main Street, #1
New Canaan, Connecticut 06840
203.966.0048
www.wadiaassociates.com

FURNITURE AND FURNISHINGS

Brunschwig & Fils
979 Third Avenue, Suite 1200
New York, New York 10022
212.838.7878
www.brunschwig.com

Christian Dior Home
30 Avenue Montaigne
Paris, France 75008
+33(0)1.40.73.73.73
www.dior.com

Christopher Spitzmiller, Inc.
248 West 35th Street, 17th Floor
New York, New York 10001
212.563.1144
www.christopherspitzmiller.com

Claremont
1059 Third Avenue, 2nd Floor
New York, New York 10065
212.486.1252
www.claremontfurnishing.com

Clarence House
979 Third Avenue, Suite 205
New York, New York 10022
212.752.2890
www.clarencehouse.com

Cowtan & Tout
979 Third Avenue, Suite 1022
New York, New York 10022
212.753.4488
www.cowtan.com

Donghia
979 Third Avenue, Suite 613
New York, New York 10022
212.935.3713
www.donghia.com

F. Schumacher & Co.
979 Third Avenue, Suite 832
New York, New York 10022
212.415.3900
www.fschumacher.com

Fortuny Inc.
979 Third Avenue, Suite 1632
New York, New York 10022
212.753.7153
www.fortuny.com

Galerie des Lampes
9 rue de Beaune
Paris, France 75007
+33(0)1.40.20.14.14
www.galeriedeslampes.com

John Matouk & Co., Inc.
11 East 26th Street
New York, New York 10010
212.683.9242
www.matouk.com

John Robshaw Textiles
245 West 29th Street, Suite 1501
New York, New York 10001
212.594.6006
www.johnrobshaw.com

John Rosselli & Associates
979 Third Avenue, Suite 1800
New York, New York 10022
212.593.2060
www.johnrosselliassociates.com

Lee Jofa
979 Third Avenue, Suite 234
New York, New York 10022
212.688.0444
www.leejofa.com

Nancy Corzine
979 Third Avenue, 8th Floor
New York, New York 10022
212.223.8340
www.nancycorzine.com

Pierre Frey
979 Third Avenue, Suite 1611
New York, New York 10022
212.421.0534
www.pierrefrey.com

Quadrille
979 Third Avenue, Suite 1415
New York, New York 10022
212.753.2995
www.quadrillefabrics.com

Robert Lighton
276 Greenpoint Avenue, Building 9,
4th Floor
Brooklyn, New York 11222
718.361.6860
www.robertlighton.com

Samuel & Sons
983 Third Avenue
New York, New York 10022
212.704.8044
www.samuelandsons.com

Scalamandre
942 Third Avenue
New York, New York 10022
212.980.3888
www.scalamandre.com

Vaughan
979 Third Avenue, Suite 1511
New York, New York 10022
212.319.7070
www.vaughandesigns.com

ANTIQUES AND VINTAGE

Bardith Ltd. Antiques
901 Madison Avenue, 1st Floor
New York, New York 10021
212.737.3775
www.bardith.com

Bern Goeckler Antiques
30 East 10th Street
New York, New York 10003
212.777.8209
www.bgoecklerantiques.com

Christie's
20 Rockefeller Plaza
New York, New York 10020
212.636.2000
www.christies.com

Daniel Barney Antiques
315 East 62nd Street, 3rd Floor
New York, New York 10021
212.755.2432
www.danielbarney.com

Dienst + Dotter, Antikviteter
411 Lafayette Street
New York, New York 10003
212.861.1200
www.dienstanddotter.com

Florian Papp Antiques
962 Madison Avenue
New York, New York 10021
212.288.6770
www.florianpapp.com

Galerie Camoin Demachy
9 Quai Voltaire
Paris, France 75007
+33(0)1.42.61.82.06
www.camoindemachyantiquaire.com

Gerald Bland Inc.
1262 Madison Avenue
New York, New York 10128
212.987.8505
www.geraldblandinc.com

Glen Dooley
78 East 11th Street
New York, New York 10003
212.995.8818
www.glendooley.com

Guinevere Antiques
574-580 Kings Road
London, UK SW6 2DY
+44(0)20.7736.2917
www.guinevere.co.uk

H. M. Luther Antiques
61 East 11th Street
New York, New York 10003
212.505.1485
www.hmluther.com

Hyde Park Antiques, Ltd.
836 Broadway
New York, New York 10003
212.477.0033
www.hydeparkantiques.com

Jonathan Burden LLC
180 Duane Street
New York, New York 10013
212.941.8247
www.jonathanburden.com

Liz O'Brien
306 East 61st Street
New York, New York 10065
212.755.3800
www.lizobrien.com

Maison Gerard
53 East 10th Street
New York, New York 10003
212.674.7611
www.maisongerard.com

Mallett
929 Madison Avenue
New York, New York 10021
212.249.8783
www.mallettantiques.com

Objets Plus Inc.
315 East 62nd Street, 3rd Floor
New York, New York 10021
212.832.3386
www.objetsplus.com

R. Louis Bofferding
970 Lexington Avenue
New York, New York 10021
212.744.6725

Soane Britain
50-52 Pimlico Road
London, UK SW1W 8LP
+44(0)20.7730.6400
www.soane.co.uk

Sotheby's
1334 York Avenue
New York, New York 10021
212.606.7000
www.sothebys.com

Todd Alexander Romano
232 East 59th Street, 4th Floor
New York, New York 10022
212.421.7722
www.toddalexanderromano.com

ART

Paul Kasmin Gallery
293 Tenth Avenue
New York, New York 10001
212.563.4474
www.paulkasmingallery.com

Rob Wynne, Artist
www.robwynne.net

ACKNOWLEDGMENTS

I want to thank my parents, Mariya and Phrixos Papachristidis, who gave me an incredible education and provided the privileges that have allowed me to have a fantastic life.

To my supportive sisters—Aurora, Thaleia, and Ophelia—whose nurturing and loving support have made me the man I am. To my brother Basil, who taught me the meaning of being a gentleman. To my beautiful sister-in-law Patrizia who is a style inspiration. To my half sisters—Helene, Marika, and Niky. To my brother-in-law Bill, who is like a brother to me, and my other brothers-in-law Neil and Robert. To my amazing nieces and nephews and their spouses: Tatina and Thomas, Phrixos and Caroline, Samantha and David, Michael and Sabrina, and Rafe.

To Scott for his steadfast love, patience, and support, and to Donna Nelson who has become part of my family.

To my dear friend Nancy Corzine, who introduced me to the wonderful editor Sandy Gilbert at Rizzoli, who believed in this book and helped me make it a reality with her remarkable skill. Thank you to Rizzoli's publisher Charles Miers for embracing this project. I am also grateful to graphic designer Doug Turshen for his vision and sense of clarity. For sharing my commitment, I want to thank the talented photographer Tria Giovan and the intuitive writer Dan Shaw. To the legendary Mario Buatta for being an inspiration and for writing the foreword. For always providing me with sound advice, I want to thank my public relations consultants and dear friends Alison Mazzola and Anna Meacham. And to Cathy Buxton, George Farias, Harry Slatkin, Liz O'Brien, and Louis Bofferding for their constant interest and support of this book.

To all of my clients and friends who graciously opened their homes to be photographed for this book: You have generous hearts. I want to make special mention of the artisans who are linchpins of my business. Cheryl and Paul Boyko, Andy Holland, Aldo Manrique, Jose Quintana, Cecilia Garzon, and Eric Englebert. My designs could not be realized without them. And a special thank you to Brigitta Williamson, who opened my first account at Brunschwig & Fils twenty-five years ago.

I am very grateful to the talented magazine editors who have encouraged me and published my work: the incomparable Margaret Russell, the divine Anita Sardisi, and the impeccable Michael Boodro.

To the women at my office who make me look good day in and day out: Thaleia Christidis, Kristin Cline, Rachel Goldberg, Nicola Hasan, Joyce Marlow, Alice Minnich, Liljana Ndoka, and Antonina Papis.

And thank you to all my other friends and clients who have supported me with unwavering love and faith. I appreciate every one of you and you know who you are.

OPPOSITE: By the fireplace in a nuanced Greenwich living room, a pair of antique wing chairs upholstered in silk damask are set in front of a Giacometti-inspired custom coffee table by Carole Gratale on a custom rug. The antique Anglo-Indian chair is upholstered in horsehair from Clarence House.